GERMANY
FOR
TRAVELERS

-The total guide-

The comprehensive traveling guide for all your traveling needs.

© 2018 by THE TOTAL TRAVEL GUIDE COMPANY
© 2018 by BRENDA PUBLISHING
All rights reserved

PUBLISHED BY

GERMANY FOR TRAVELERS

Table of Contents

Why do we claim our guides are "total guides"?

Chapter 1: This is Germany

Chapter 2: A trip through history

Chapter 3: Discovering the tasteful side of Germany

Chapter 4: Germany through the year

Chapter 5: Germany's scenic and tourist routes

Chapter 6: Transportation and getting around Germany

Chapter 7: Germany's liveliest festivals

Chapter 8: The best dining in Germany

Chapter 9: Germany after dark & best clubs for dancing the night away

Chapter 10: Exploring Germany's top cities and attractions

Chapter 11: Where to stay - Best hotels and hostels

Chapter 12: Amazing small towns in Germany and popular travel destinations

Chapter 13: Important things everyone should know

Chapter 14: Final Words

Why do we claim our guides are "total guides"?

Why are they really comprehensive?

Because we do almost anything to make sure that all the main issues relevant to the conscious traveler are covered in our guides.

We hate the typical boring travel guides chocked up with standard information you can readily find on the Internet.

We travel, we research other guides, we talk to locals, we ask friends, we ask friends of friends,

we do whatever it takes to make sure that we have you covered. All the angles! This is how we get the best tips, the most valuable for every one of our travel destinations.

That is where we got the best tips, the most valuable ones about our travel destinations.

All our guides are reviewed and edited by a "local" writer to make sure that the guide is one of its kind, comprehensive, fun and interesting. We prefer not to add too many maps or photos since you can have all that on the internet. We prefer to focus the content on tips and unique data that makes worthwhile to buy our total guides.

We use different approaches for each city, as each destination is unique. You will be able to verify that our guides are not standardized. Each one is different because each place is different. And you will enjoy the difference,

Our production team is very proud of our guides. We hope you will enjoy the reading and take full advantage of your traveling.   !

Chapter 1: This is Germany

Germany is one of the most fascinating and appealing countries in Europe. It is a country in west-central Europe, that stretches from the Alps, across the North European Plain to the North Sea and the Baltic Sea. It has the second largest population in Europe. Compared with Australia or Canada, Germany is a fairly small country. The main rivers in Germany are the famous Rhine, the Elbe, and the Danube, one of Europe's longest rivers.

Germany has a wealth of interesting historical sites, festivals, sporting attractions, world-class restaurants, a whole range of museums and more than 30 UNESCO World Heritage Sites. These range from sites of natural beauty like the Messel Pit to cultural riches such as the Cologne Cathedral and the Zollverein industrial complex in Nordrhein-Westfalen. Germany also has some delightful places which often aren't on the main tourist map, from vast mountain ranges, steaming rivers to sweeping coastlines. With breathtaking scenery, sensational culture, and historic sites it's no wonder people leave their hearts here.

Germany firmly holds its position as the leading country in Europe, and consistently ranks among the biggest producers of iron, cement, chemicals, machinery, automobiles, and electronics in the world. Not surprisingly, since Germany is one of the world's largest economies. As the birthplace of Johann Sebastian Bach, Ludwig van Beethoven, Johann Wolfgang von Goethe, and Immanuel Kant, among others, Germany is a country with some of the greatest contributions to world culture, literature, technology, philosophy, and music. It is also a country of stunning and diverse natural beauty.

Germany is undeniably one of the world's greatest countries. It shares borders with 9 countries, more than any other European country; Denmark in the north, Poland and the Czech Republic in the east, Switzerland and Austria in the south, France in the southwest and Belgium, Luxembourg and the Netherlands in the west. The country covers an area of 357,021 square kilometres and has 16 federal states - each unique and with a lot of things to offer. The states are known as *Bundesländer*. Since Germany has a federal constitution, each state has its own state constitution.

This wonderful country has a lot to offer; unforgettable scenery, friendly people, opportunities to enjoy a huge range of activities, entertainment of all kinds, and historic sites to explore. Germany has a number of large cities, such as Berlin, Hamburg, Munich, Cologne, Frankfurt, and Stuttgart. Berlin, Hamburg and Bremen are often called city-states.

Chapter 2: A trip through history

Germany has a long and rich history. The country was occupied first by the Roman Empire, then the Holy Roman Empire and finally the Austrian Habsburgs. However, the area becomes associated with the name Germany in the 1st century BC, when Julius Caesar conquered the Roman province of Gaul. The Germanic tribes inhabited the northern part of the European continent since 500 B.C. It was a long process, but Otto I, finally managed to unite the German states in 962. The events from the 16th century have a major significance in our history. In 1571, Martin Luther, a professor of theology at Wittenberg University in Saxony, posted 95 theses on the door of the Wittenberg Castle church. He brought on the Protestant Reformation with his criticism of the Catholic Church, a movement that sparked the Thirty Years' War.

The Holy Roman Empire fought several wars before the Peace of Westphalia in 1648. The fall of the Holy Roman Empire in 1806 had drastic consequences for Germany. In 1862, Otto von Bismarck became President Minister of Prussia. He defeated Denmark and Austria in 1866. Germany then became a federal state with a national parliament.

Otto von Bismarck involved Germany in a series of alliances to isolate France, Germany's biggest enemy. Tensions in other areas caused by Germany's foreign policies erupt into World War I. And as a result, Germany was defeated.

At the beginning of the 20th century, Adolf Hitler's Nazi Party took advantage of the discontent existing in the country. In January 1933, he was appointed as the chancellor of Germany, and the Weimar Republic became a one-party state. The blackest moment in the history started when Adolf Hitler and his followers attempted to exterminate the entire Jewish population of Europe. The Night of Broken Glass marks the actual beginning of the Holocaust. In 1938, it took place throughout the German Reich on 9-10 November. Many Jews were murdered, thousands and thousands of Jewish houses and shops were devastated and completely destroyed, many synagogues were set on fire and thousands of windows were broken.

In September 1939, Hitler attacked Poland, which led to war with Britain and France, and World War II. The war ended six years later, in spring 1945, with Germany's capitulation. The country was divided into occupation zones, each under the control of one ally. In 1949, the West part of Germany became the Federal Republic of Germany, while the Soviet zone became the German Democratic Republic, a communist state.

Germany begins a period of fast economic growth and development. In 1961 the Berlin Wall was built, dividing the city in two. In the end, on 9 November 1989, the Berlin Wall fell. In 1991, after a long period of time, Germany was finally reunited.

Chapter 3: Discovering the tasteful side of Germany

German cuisine may not be highly celebrated around the world, however **thanks to Germany's incredible markets, diverse ethnic influences, and internationally acclaimed chefs, it is** not hard to be impressed by the food on offer at some of the finest restaurants in the country. German cuisine **varies greatly from region to region, and each region has its own speciality dish. It is no longer fashionable to claim that German food is plain and simple. German food is rich and delicious.**

The country has a lot of traditional restaurants to choose from, each serving their own unique modern interpretations of the country's traditional dishes. The most popular herbs used in our cuisine are parsley, thyme, laurel, chives, black pepper, juniper berries, nutmeg, cinnamon, cardamom and caraway. German mustard is often used in food preparation, but our dishes are rarely hot and spicy.

One of the most popular dishes in Germany is *Apfelstrudel.* Apple strudel or *Apfelstrudel* is a traditional Viennese strudel, but it's so popular in Germany. Basically, it is a delicious pastry filled with apples. The filling is made of grated cooking apples, sugar, cinnamon, raisins, and bread crumbs. It's served

15

warm and sprinkled with powdered sugar. Cheesecake, ice cream and sorbets are also very popular in Germany.

The Black Forest cake or *Schwarzwälder Kirschtorte* is the most famous dessert in the country. It consists of several layers of chocolate cake, filled with whipped cream or butter cream and cherries. It is the most popular specialty from the Black Forest region.

Rote Grütze is a sweet fruit pudding made of black and red currants, raspberries and sometimes strawberries or cherries. It is served hot or cold as a dessert with milk, vanilla sauce or whipped cream.

Kartoffelpuffer are shallow-fried pancakes made of grated or ground potato, mixed with flour, egg, onion and seasoning. These pancakes may be topped with a variety of condiments. Bread is also a significant part of our cuisine.

Spätzle are noodles made from wheat flour and egg. They are often served topped with cheese.

Germany is a paradise for meat lovers. Whether its steak, sausage, ribs or burgers, Germany has it. *Eintopf* is a traditional type of German stew. The name of this dish literally means 'one pot' and refers to a simple way of cooking all ingredients in one pot. *Wurst* is a significant part of our cuisine. More than 1500 different types of sausage are made in Germany.

Among the most popular are the *Bratwurst*, made of ground pork and spices, and the *Currywurst,* made of steamed, then fried pork sausage and spiced with curry ketchup. I can't recommend it strongly enough.

Sauerbraten is one of the national dishes of Germany. Basically, it is a pot roast that can be prepared with different types of meat, most often beef. Variations also include *Sauerbraten* of pork. This dish is usually served with potato dumplings, braised cabbage, and apple sauce.

A *schnitzel* is a thin, boneless meat, coated with flour, beaten eggs and bread crumbs. It is often served with a slice of lemon. There are many variations of the dish, depending on your tastes. As you can see, German cuisine is a rich palette of tastes with a distinct traditional character. Hopefully you will get a taste of the country's culinary delicacies.

Chapter 4: Germany through the year

Germany is a year-round destination, with an exceedingly varied landscape, and the weather usually adds to the country's charm. It's a temperate country with cold, wet winters and moderate warm summers. However, Germany's climate is dominated by several geographical factors: the Alps, the sea, the rivers, the valleys, and the forests. The weather conditions in Germany are usually very unpredictable, and each region has its own weather patterns.

In the northwest and far north the climate is extremely oceanic and generally predictable, with rainfall expected all year round. Summers are generally warm with moderately high rainfall, and winters are relatively mild and cloudy. January is usually the coldest month.

In the east, winters can be very cold and harsh, and summers are generally very warm, while the south has a transitional climate. Winters there are mild and summers tend to be cool, although the temperature can change quite rapidly during the day. The Alpine regions in the extreme south have a mountain climate which is characterized by lower temperatures and occasional warm *föhn* wind. The weather in central Germany can vary considerably. Winters are usually cold and summers tend to be warm.

Germany does have plenty of good weather, contrary to most people's beliefs. The country is especially beautiful in the spring, and the blossoms and flowers bring Germany to life between April and May. Spring in Germany is a fantastic time to check out the country's beautiful mountains, lowlands, and parks, or to indulge in leisurely strolls. However, it can be quite crowded at this time of year. Autumn is also a very good time to visit Germany. While temperatures are a little cooler than summer, the weather is still pleasant.

Winter brings colder weather to much of the country, but with so much to do and see in Germany, even rainy days can be beautiful. Summer is an excellent time for hiking, camping and a variety of other outdoor activities. Germany's beautiful beaches are ideal for swimming, sunbathing, surfing, sailing, and water sports. Germany makes a great holiday destination at any time of the year, but the countryside is at its most attractive from April to the end of October.

Chapter 5: Germany's scenic and tourist routes

Germany is home to a great collection of scenic routes and inspirational views. The country has over 100 thematic and scenic routes, from the Romantic Road to the Castle Road. Driving is the best way to discover the most spectacular scenery of Germany. Be sure to visit the Black forest and Leipzig which gives a taste of old Europe. Visiting numerous castles and churches lining the route is half the fun as you make your way from one quaint town to the next.

The Castle Road is one of Germany's oldest scenic routes. More than 70 fortresses, castles and palaces along the route are well worth your time and attention. The Castle route runs for almost 1200 km from the city of Mannheim to the historic city of Prague. There is no better way to immerse yourself in a world of castles, medieval towns and romance as well as beautiful countryside. Highlights on the route include the lovely Mannheim Palace, and the magnificent Neuenstein Castle. This route takes you through some of the most beautiful places in Germany, and through a series of lovely medieval towns, while enjoying some of the most spectacular scenery in the country.

If I had to recommend only one scenic route in the country, it would definitely be the Romantic Road. The Romantic Road runs from Würzburg to Füssen in southern Germany. This route is 350 kilometres long and one of Germany's most popular scenic routes for over 60 years. As well as proffering wonderful views of the varied landscapes of the Main river, you can also see the picturesque Lechfeld, and the tranquil Pfaffenwinkel region. In addition, you will pass through a number of picturesque towns, villages and attractive castles. This route offers an unforgettable experience for everyone, and boasts some of the most magnificent scenery in Germany.

Another route worth mentioning is the Fairy Tale Route. The route runs from Hanau in central Germany to Bremen in the north. With a length of 600 kilometres, the route will let you explore the magical world of the Brothers Grimm, fairy tales, myths and legends. This route passes through various scenic regions, which include eight nature parks. Along the route, visitors can see numerous picturesque medieval towns, enchanting castles and fortresses, the House of Little Red Riding Hood and a Snow White Museum. The Fairy Tale Route pinpoints many of the historic places that make this picturesque region and its valleys, a truly majestic place.

One of the most interesting routes is the Old Salt Route. It was one of the most frequently used trade routes in the Middle Ages. The route functioned as an important connection between the northern and southern parts of the country. The route runs for approximately 100 km from the town of Lüneberg, to the Hanseatic town of Lübeck, gateway to the Baltic Sea. It is especially attractive for nature lovers and history buffs. Numerous magnificent sights line the old trade route, including the Lüne Monastery, the scenic Lüneburg Heath Nature Park, and the Sachsenwald Forest. Other locations include many romantic towns, and small villages with splendid town halls.

Chapter 6: Transportation and getting around Germany

Germany has a very dense and modern transport infrastructure. To be honest, it has one of the finest public transport systems in Europe. Germany probably has one of the most advanced transportation systems in the world.

Germany's public transportation is both efficient and convenient. One of the most popular ways to get around Germany is to rent a car. Car rentals are available all around the country. The biggest advantage of using a car is that you can wander away from the main roads and discover the real Germany. However, since Germany is well served by public transportation and taxis, having a car is not essential to visit the country.

One of the most enjoyable ways to get around is by bicycle. Bike paths allow cyclists to explore various treasures in the country. Since drivers are not always attentive, you should always be alert. Bike rental is also widely available in cities.

Taxis are a great way to see the country, however, they can often be a costly way to travel. Taxis are metered and charged at a base rate, plus a per-kilometre fee.

Available taxis have rooftop lights lit, but it is nearly imppossible to flag down a taxi in Germany. You can usually find them at the edge of the pedestrian centres.

For the most part, bus travel is the most cost effective way to travel around the country, and nearly all towns have their own comprehensive network. Standard tickets are priced according to the distance travelled. Obviously, tickets must be validated upon boarding in order to be valid. You can buy your tickets on board, at the Reisezentrum or travel centre and from various vending machines with English instructions.

Frankfurt, Stuttgart, Hannover, Cologne, and some other cities, have a light rail system, commonly known as a *Stadtbahn*. The stations are usually marked with the standard "U" U-Bahn sign with the word "Stadtbahn".

In the larger cities you can find a full-fledged subway system, or U-Bahn. U-Bahn stations are marked with the standard "U" sign, followed by the number. Cities with U-Bahn systems are Berlin, Munich, Hamburg, Nuremberg, Frankfurt and Stuttgart. The frequency of trains usually fluctuates.

The largest urban cities like Berlin, Hamburg, Munich, Frankfurt-Mainz-Wiesbaden, Stuttgart, Cologne, Düsseldorf, Nuremburg, Dresden, and Magdeburg, have a superb suburban train system called the S-Bahn. S-

Bahn stations are distinguished with the standard "S" sign.

The above mentioned methods of travel are the most popular, but they are not the only ways to get around. You may want to consider walking to your destination. Each method of travel is effective. Cruise ships also run on the Main River between Mainz and Frankfurt; on the Danube from Nürnberg to Linz in Austria, going on to Vienna and Budapest; and on the Mosel between Cochem and Trier. From Hamburg, you can easily reach the cities in Northern Germany. Lübeck and Bremen are only a short train ride away. From Munich and Berlin, you can easily reach some extraordinary places in the Bavarian Alps, including Garmisch-Partenkirchen, Nuremberg, and Lindau.

Airports in Germany

Most tourists arrive in Germany by either train or plane. Practically all German cities with commercial airports have an airport shuttle service. Frankfurt Airport is Germany's largest airport which ranks among the world's top ten airports. It is a major transportation hub in Europe, with the biggest number of international destinations served worldwide. The Airport is situated 12 km southwest of central Frankfurt, near the Autobahn intersection Frankfurter

Kreuz. To reach the city center, you can rent a car, take a taxi, ride the bus, or travel by train. The journey usually takes around 30 minutes.

Berlin has several airports, but Tegel airport is much closer to the city centre than Schoenefeld. Tegel Airport is the main international airport in the city. It is located in Tegel, approximately 8 km northwest of the city centre of Berlin. The best way to reach the city centre is to take one of the Airport Express buses. Buses run approximately every 10 minutes, and you can purchase your ticket either directly from the driver, from any ticket machine outside the terminal building or at the ticket counter.

The Bavarian capital is home to the second busiest airport in Germany. Munich Airport is located 30 km northeast of Munich near the city of Freising. The airport is served by S-Bahn rail service and bus, so it has a direct S-Bahn railway link to the city. The journey takes around 45 minutes. Tickets can be purchased at the ticket counter in the central area between the two terminals, or from any ticket machine.

Stuttgart Airport is one of the top ten busiest airports in the country. It serves more than nine million passengers each year. The airport is located approximately 13 km south of Stuttgart. The airport is well served by Stuttgart's public transport system, and the rail system. It takes less than 30 minutes to reach the city centre.

Hamburg Airport, also known as Hamburg-Fuhlsbüttel Airport, is located 8.5 km north of Hamburg, in the Fuhlsbüttel quarter. It is the fifth-busiest airport in the country. The airport is served by S-Bahn rail service, and the journey takes around 30 minutes. Cologne Bonn Airport, also known as Flughafen Köln-Wahn, is one of the largest commercial airports in the country. The airport is located in the district of Porz, approximately 14.8 km southeast of the city centre.

Chapter 7: Germany's liveliest festivals

Germany has a lot of festivals. And when I say a lot, I mean a lot. With more than 10000 festivals celebrated across the country, Germany has something for every taste and interest. And the nightlife in Germany will not disappoint you either. In most cities in Germany you can visit a few good festivals throughout the year.

One of the best festivals in the world doesn't need an introduction. The Munich Oktoberfest, also known as the "Wiesn" is the world's largest annual beer festival for nearly 200 years. This famous festival runs for 16 days usually from late September to the first weekend in October. The festival is held in an area named the Theresienwiese, located near Munich's center and attracts over six million visitors each year. People flock from all over the world to participate in the celebration.

You can find many events during this festival, showcasing some of the best local traditions and customs. There are outdoor food stalls, beer tasting, amusement rides, sidestalls and games, and a wide variety of traditional food. The festival celebrates all that is good about Germany.

Berlin is also known for its plethora of seemingly random festivals. The Berlin International Film Festival, also called the Berlinale, is the second largest film festival in the world after Cannes. The Berlinale is one of the city's most important annual events. The festival showcases a wide variety of films from all over the world, and attracts the elite of the film industry. Founded in 1951, only six years after the end of the Second World War, the festival is a must-do for serious movie buffs. With over 300,000 tickets sold, the festival attracts the biggest audience and delivers the biggest reward for movie enthusiasts. Tickets can be hard to find sometimes, but the best way to purchase your tickets is through the festival's website. In addition, the Berlinale hosts a large number of workshops and special events.

With more than 3000 events held at 350 difference venues, the Leipzig Book Fair is the second largest book fair in the country after the Frankfurt Book Fair. It is one of the most important events of international literature, and a great opportunity to meet other authors or editors. It is also the perfect place to socialise and exchange ideas. The festival takes place annually at the Leipzig Trade Fairground in the northern part of Leipzig.

As a country famed for its traditional culture and classical music, Germany has something to suit every taste. Each year thousands of visitors flock to Germany to dance the day and night away. The Hurricane Festival is everything a music festival should be. The festival takes place in Scheeßel, a small town between Hamburg and Bremen. It is held annually, usually every June. The Hurricane features rock, indie, and electro subgenres, and if you want to party like there is no tomorrow, Scheeße is where you belong.

These are just some of the largest festivals. In the summer you can find a festival almost every weekend. However, it is advisable to purchase your festival passes as early as possible.

Chapter 8: The best dining in Germany

Germany's dining scene is as diverse as its visitors with restaurants serving mouth-watering food from around the world. With so many different cultures in Germany, you can find some amazing dishes from almost any culture you wish. The country has a number of fine dining restaurants offering superb German cuisine in plush environments. You can also find plenty of fast food outlets throughout the country, and lots of places selling takeout food, where you can buy deep-fried fish, hamburgers, sausages, chips, sandwiches, or pizza.

Berlin

Berlin is the top culinary destination in Germany. The city is packed with restaurants and eateries that won't empty your wallet. Start with dinner at Hugos Restaurant. It is one of the best restaurants in Berlin. The restaurant is awarded with 17 Gault Millau points and a Michelin star, and offers a haute cuisine dining experience in an elegant setting. The restaurant perfectly combines international and regional flavours. It is very popular with business people who work in

the neighbourhood. Hugos is located at the top of the Inter-Continental Hotel.
(Address: Budapester Str. 2/14. Etage, 10787 Berlin)

Of course, there are thousands and thousands of restaurants in the city, but you can't leave Berlin without eating Wurst—you can't. Currywurst and Bockwurst are found everywhere, but the best place to stuff yourself with some cheap eats including currywurst, fried burgers and buletten is Curry 36. It's a party every night at this popular stand, and even if you have to stand in line for a while, it is worth it.
(Address: Mehringdamm 36, 10961 Berlin)

Jolesch is one of the few places in the area where you will find good, reasonably priced meals to enjoy in an attractive atmosphere. Its beautiful decor creates a soothing and relaxing atmosphere, and the menu features a wide variety of flavours. In addition, the wine list will definitely please connoisseurs. This charming little Austrian restaurant is located in a quirky corner of Kreuzberg.
(Address: Muskauer Str. 1, 10997 Berlin)

Munich

The Bavarian capital is home to numerous restaurants, and it can actually be quite hard to choose because each restaurant has its own culinary identity. The city has plenty of delicious options to satisfy every taste and budget, and offers an eclectic mix of dining experiences. There are really plenty of places to grab a bite in Munich, but when you are ready to sample our cuisine, head to one of the best restaurants in the city. Dallmayr restaurant and coffee house is a two-star Michelin restaurant situated in one of Munich's premier delicatessens. This restaurant lives up to its reputation as one of the best restaurants in the city. Menus change often, but you should try their lamb filled with bell pepper. They also boast an extensive wine list, just be sure to book a table well in advance.

(Address: Dienerstrasse 14-15 | 80331 Munich, 80331)

If your itinerary is planned around the heart of Munich's Marienplatz, head to Acquarello. It is the only Michelin starred Italian restaurant in the city and has an attractive leafy terrace. It is a distinguished spot for a great meal in a lively setting. A variety of pasta offerings round out the menu. The restaurant is often filled with locals, and reservations are recommended. (Address: Mühlbaurstraße 36, 81677 Munich)

Buffet Kull is one of the best dining establishments in the city. The food is excellent, and the menu is a mix of French and German influences and includes several surprises, such as the famous New York steak. Friendly service in a charming setting guarantee a positive culinary experience.

(Address: Marienstraße 4, 80331 Munich)

Hamburg

Hamburg is known for its plethora of traditional restaurants that make this fair city unique. And each restaurant has many unique tastes to offer for your pleasure. Le Canard Nouveau is without a doubt one of the best restaurants in Hamburg and a good choice for a business lunch. This Michelin-starred restaurant is situated on a hill and offers an amazing panoramic view of the harbour and the Elbe River. Le Canard Nouveau serves a refreshingly creative variety of dishes in an elegant setting.
(Address: Elbchaussee 139, 22763 Hamburg)

Set over three floors, the Restaurant Nil will rock your senses with tantalizing food. It is a wonderful spot to savour our traditional dishes, but the menu also features an array of choices for any taste or appetite. The restaurant is well known for its excellent, deliciously refined cuisine, and the service is very attentive.
(Address: Neuer Pferdemarkt 5, Hamburg)

If you are looking for a cheap and tasty bite in Hamburg, head to Erika's Eck. Located in the trendy neighborhood of Sternschanze, this restaurant offers a wide choice of traditional dishes. The restaurant serves

probably the best schnitzels in the area, as well as a number of other specialties.
(Address: Sternstraße 98, 20357 Hamburg)

Stuttgart

Stuttgart has many restaurants that will satisfy your appetite. The city's restaurant scene has been expanding for so many years, which explains why so many visitors want to experience the spectacle for themselves. When it's time to dine, you will have plenty of options. The city is a foodie's paradise. If you are looking for something out of the ordinary, head to one of my favorite eateries in Stuttgart. Olivo is a Michelin-starred restaurant at the five-star Steigenberger Graf Zeppelin hotel. This Italian restaurant is a real gem. Considered by many as one of Stuttgart's best restaurants, Olivo is the definition of fine dining.

(Address: Arnulf-Klett-Platz 7, 70173 Stuttgart)

A haven for meat-lovers, Tauberquelle is known for its hearty, delicious dishes. It is a lively place, to say the least. Generous portions of Swabian food are served at this friendly restaurant. Its menu offers a wide choice of interesting dishes, and the wine selection is exceptional.
(Address: Torstraße 19, 70173 Stuttgart)

There is an enormous choice of places to eat in the center, and you will have no trouble finding an ice-cream parlors in Stuttgart, they are everywhere. But I have to admit, Eiscafe Old Bridge Gelateria is my personal favorite. It offers a range of fancy ice creams with creative flavors.
(Address: Bolzstraße 10, 70173 Stuttgart)

Frankfurt

There is a restaurant for everyone in Frankfurt. The city has many restaurants ranging from small eateries to full scale restaurants. With hundreds of restaurants throughout the area, it is really hard to know where to begin.

A Lebanese restaurant in Frankfurt? Why not! L'emir is my favorite restaurant in Frankfurt. It is possibly one of the hippest eateries in the city. The food is fantastic and, although the restaurant is not inexpensive, it offers a very good value for the money. The music is loud, the atmosphere lively, and you can see an impressive belly dance performances every Friday and Saturday night.
(Address: Weserstraße 17, 60329 Frankfurt am Main)

The Main Tower Restaurant & Lounge is unlike any other restaurant in Frankfurt. It is one of the most romantic and popular fine-dining establishments the

area. The Main Tower Restaurant & Lounge serves delicious and resolutely hearty international cuisine, and offers a spectacular view of the city. A modern setting defi nitely plays a role in attracting the restaurant's clientele. The restaurant also has an extensive wine list.
(Address: Neue Mainzer Str. 52-58, 60311 Frankfurt am Main)

Pizzeria Romanella is perfect for anyone on a tight budget. This is a friendly restaurant located in the heart of the city. It is always packed with locals and tourists. The menu consists of a reliable choice of standard dishes, and the food is simply sensational. (Address: Wolfsgangstraße 84, 60322 Frankfurt am Main)

Chapter 9: Germany after dark & best clubs for dancing the night away

From sundown until early morning, Germany is always alive. You can find numerous nightclubs designed to suit everyone's tastes. Berlin, Munich, Stuttgart, Hamburg and Frankfurt are some of the coolest cities in Germany when it comes to nightlife, boasting a huge selection of bars and clubs. It is time to start discovering Germany's nightlife. And let's start with Berlin. Berlin's reputation as a vibrant, lively and unique city is well established. It is definitely the best clubbing city in Europe. It has a thriving complex of bars and clubs, and Berlin never truly shuts down. Some of the most popular clubs in the city are located in the districts of Kreuzberg und Friedrichshain. You will feel right at home in this unassuming area. You can start the night at Berghain. It is one of the world's best nightclubs, and is jam-packed on weekends. The club has two dance floors, and is regarded as one of the best techno clubs in the world. The club is housed in an old industrial warehouse and has a distinctly laid-back atmosphere. If you are more into deep house, head to Watergate. It is one of the hippest nightlife addresses in Berlin, where DJs like Eric Morillo, and Adam

Freeland are common guests. The club has a more sophisticated appeal, with a laid-back atmosphere.

Berlin also has some of the best bars in Germany. If you are looking for something a little more relaxed, head to Max und Moritz. Located in the heart of the Kreuzberg district, Max und Moritz is one of the busiest bars and restaurants in the area since 1902. It has a library and a private dining room, and provides a unique and welcoming atmosphere with its elegant setting.

One thing is certain, the Bavarian capital has something for everyone. Munich is a fascinating city. As you might expect, the city has a massive selection of clubs, pubs, and bars, but there are some hotspots that always guarantee a memorable night. You can find more than 20 clubs, pubs, bars and several concert stages, all in one spot. The Kultfabrik is the former dumpling factory and houses the largest selection of clubs in the city. The music here includes every imaginable style: garage, rock, pop, surf, alternative, techno-industrial, as well as Schweinerock. You can immerse yourself in the atmosphere of Munich in P1 Club, before heading off to another trendy spot. P1 Club is the place to be seen and one of Munich's premier nightclubs. The music varies from electro hits to house and funk. The center of the club is lined with dance floors and six bars.

One of the main go-to bars in the city is Negroni Bar. This trendy bar has a large selection of 140 cocktails on offer. This is a popular spot so make sure to come early to get a seat. This bar features some of the best cocktails that Munich has to offer.

Hamburg regularly attracts some of the world's best and most successful DJs. As with any city in Germany, it has its fair share of bars, pubs and nightclubs. The city features one of Germany's most thriving and exciting nightlife scenes. The most popular place in the city for fans of sports and beer is probably the Irish Rover. It is a real pub located in the heart of the city, and offers a wide selection of sandwiches and salads, and an even wider range of Irish whiskeys. The Irish Rover is that place where everybody knows your name.

When it comes to clubs in Hamburg, Grosse Freiheit 36 is one of the coolest places in the city, famous for its modern live concerts. Several big names in the music industry have performed here, including Iggy Pop, and the Beatles.

Stuttgart also has numerous bars, inviting cafes, and nightclubs packed with friendly people. Whatever your preference, you are pretty much guaranteed to find it here. The area around Theodor-Heuss-Strasse is lined with popular nightclubs and bars. One of the most famous clubs in the city is Muttermilch. The club has a slightly retro feel, a good-sized dance floor and a chill-out corner. The music varies from soul hits to house and funk. With new clubs and cafes popping up seemingly every day it is hard to decide where to go. While you are here, be sure to check out the Waranga Bar. It is a modern bar located right in the heart of the city, at the Schlossplatz. The bar is extremely popular, especially in the summer months.

Frankfurt is known for its vibrant and lively nightlife. The city offers a wide array of activities to choose from. Whether you are looking for a place to unwind or dance until the wee hours of the morning, you will find it all here. Be forewarned, these clubs are tremendously popular and often very crowded. Many bars in the city offer live music, especially around Kleine Bockenheimer Strasse. Harveys is one of the best places in the city to grab a drink. This trendy bar is very popular, and occasionally features live disco bands. You can dance the night away at APT-Apartment. It is one the city's hottest clubs. The music ranges from funk, house and acid jazz, with famous DJs passing through regularly. The club also has a chill-out corner.

Chapter 10: Exploring Germany's top cities and attractions

You may be wondering where to go and what to see in Germany, especially if you've never been here before. Although the main cities are the most popular destinations, I also encourage you to at least check fares to the smaller destinations. The country has a lot of cities and villages, and they are all unique and special in their own ways. It is important to make decisions about where you want to go based on your preferences. Germany is a great country, especially for long-term travelers. The number of cities, and villages in such a small geographical area gives you the opportunity to explore a variety of attractions and amenities during a long-term trip. After all, the number of cities and places you visit depends on how much time you have available. Luckily, in each of the cities there is plenty to do and see. However, if you are planning a trip to this country; Berlin, Munich, Hamburg, Stuttgart and Frankfurt are some of the best cities to visit.

A portrait of Eastern Germany: Berlin

Berlin is the capital city of the Federal Republic of Germany and a significant center of Europe. With a population of 3.5 million people, Berlin is Germany's largest city. Besides being the capital city, Berlin is also one of the three city states among the 16 states of Germany.

Berlin has an impressive array of wineries. Visitors will enjoy exploring picturesque rivers and lakes, forests and gardens. Berlin is commonly called the heart of Germany, and literally overflows with sightseeing options. Berlin is located on the banks of Rivers Spree and Havel in Eastern Germany, and offers a wide range of attractions and activities for visitors. The city is home to renowned universities, theatres and museums. It is also well known for its festivals, gardens, diverse architecture, restaurants, nightlife, its relaxed elegant charm, and a high quality of living. Berlin is undoubtely one of the most cosmopolitan cities in the world, but it has compelling appeal in its parks and lakes, its historical buildings, its character and its endless charm. An important part of Berlin's cultural world is its vibrant theatre scene, and most of the major houses can be found in the central Mitte district.

A stroll through modern Berlin is step back in time. Those interested in history should definitely visit the Museum Island. It is the museum complex of five world-renowned museums built between 1824 and 1930. The area is home to some of the most valued cultural treasures in the country.

The Museum Island is one of the most interesting places in the German capital, and in 1999, the complex was added to the UNESCO list of World Heritage Sites. The star of the museum complex is definitely the Pergamon, which houses many historically significant buildings such as the Pergamon Altar, the Market Gate of Miletus, and the Ishtar Gate of Babylon. The Pergamon also contains an impressive antiquity collection, an Islamic art collection, and a Middle East collection.

The Reichstag building is one of Berlin's most historic landmarks. The building was opened in 1894 to house the Imperial Diet of the German Empire. This architectural landmark was completely restored after the reunification of Germany, and eventually turned into the home of Germany's parliament. The massive glass dome at the very top of this imposing building has a 360 degree view of Berlin and its surroundings. Admission is free, but you need to register online in advance.

In the nearby area you can also find a number of government buildings, such as the German Federal Chancellery and the Brandenburg Gate. The Brandenburg Gate is one of the most famous landmarks in Germany. Built in 1791, this imposing structure served as a symbol of both the division of the country and Germany's reunification. The gate is decorated with beautiful reliefs and sculptures. Located on the western edge of Pariser Platz, the Brandenburg Gate is also one of the biggest public areas in Berlin and the main venue for various celebrations.

Among Berlin's many attractions, the city's architecture has a charm that draws visitors to its neighbourhoods. The Fernsehturm is a television tower located in the heart of Berlin in Alexanderplatz. Built in the 1960s, the tower has become one of the most famous symbols of the country. With its height of 368 meters, this tower is the tallest building in the city and offers its visitors a 360 degree panorama view of Berlin. It is one of the most prominent symbols of Germany.

Another important place to visit is the Gedenkstätte Berliner Mauer which commemorates the division of the city by the Berlin Wall after the Second World War and the deaths that occurred there. The Berlin Wall

Memorial is located on Bernauer Straße at the corner of Ackerstraße.

Berlin is a huge city, and you can find just about anything you want. The city has more than 50 shopping centres. But don't expect to find many bargains. The

Kurfürstendamm, also known as Ku'damm is one of the most famous avenues in the city. This very broad and long avenue is full of shops, boutiques, and high-end brands including Chanel, Prada and Louis Vuitton. You can also find more affordable options such as Mango, H&M, and C&A. This avenue has everything to please both window-shoppers and big spenders. Another street worth mentioning is the Tauentzienstrasse. It is a major shopping street and home to Peek and Cloppenburg and KaDeWe, continental Europe's largest department store. The street is lined with cafes and restaurants.

Berlin also has some amazing malls. The Alexa shopping mall with its 56,000 square metres is one of the largest shopping centres in the city. This mall features a wide array of shops including Mediamarkt, Zara, Esprit, H&M, Tommy Hillfiger, Quicksilver, and Mango. There is also a cinema and the LOXX model train exhibition. The Alexa shopping mall is located near Alexanderplatz.

Shoppers, this is a necessary stop. The Mall of Berlin is the largest shopping mall in Berlin. It is located between Potsdamer Platz and Friedrichstraße. The mall has 270 stores and offers a great selection of some of the best fashion brands including Massimo, Armani Jeans, Swarovski, Lacoste, Desigual, Intersport, Lacoste, Levi's, Esprit, Mango, Max & Co, Mexx, Navyboot, Nike, Guess, and Tommy Hilfiger. The mall also has a range of coffee shops, fast food outlets and around 50 restaurants.

Brandenburg

Brandenburg lies in the east of the country. The main rivers in the state are the Spree and the Havel. Its capital is Potsdam. Brandenburg is known for its well-preserved natural environment. And if you are particularly attracted by outdoor activities, visiting Brandenburg from spring to autumn is probably the best time, as you have access to all trails. Its varied terrain offers plenty of activities, including hiking and trekking.

Potsdam is the capital of Brandenburg and is well known for its castles and historic buildings. However, numerous buildings have been destroyed during the Second World War. The city is worth at least a brief visit, as there is much to see. Most of the tourist attractions in Potsdam are UNESCO World Heritage sites. The city also has an excellent range of shops, restaurants, pubs, clubs, plus all types of accommodation.

Potsdam has several interesting museums that are filled with informative and valuable exhibits, such as the Museum of Natural History and the Film Museum. The Museum of Natural History takes you on a journey through Brandenburg's animal kingdom and has many permanent exhibition's sections. On the other hand, the Film Museum is dedicated to the famous Babelsberg Film Studios. It is housed in one of the oldest buildings in the city. This Baroque building was used to accommodate the royal carriages and horses.

If your time is limited, make sure you visit the Sanssouci Park. It offers a tranquil oasis among the hustle and bustle. This beautiful park is on the UNESCO World Heritage list. The park is home to several palaces, temples, fountains, greenhouses and pavilions, and features an impressive garden with lawns, bushes, flower beds, hedges and trees. The park is easily accessible by public transportation or car.

The Sanssouci Palace is notable for the numerous temples, verdant gardens and terraced vineyards in the park. It was built between 1745 and 1747 for the Prussian king. The area is perfect for exploring, walking or for just wandering around. Another fascinating place to visit is the New Palace, situated on the western side of the Sanssouci park. Built in 1769, this beautiful palace is considered to be the last great

Prussian palace. It is the largest and most impressive palace in the area.

Nearby are the Temple of Friendship and the Antique Temple. The Temple of Friendship was built by the Prussian king Frederick II. It was dedicated to his beloved sister, Markgravine Wilhelmine of Bayreuth. The Antique Temple was built in 1768 as a complement to the Temple of Friendship.

This beautiful city is a haven for nature enthusiasts and history buffs. Its streets still have their medieval layout, and the center is very compact, and easy to explore. Visitors can spend their days walking around the picturesque south bank of lake Griebnitz. You can also visit the old market in the historic city center. There are also plenty of interesting neighbourhoods to explore, such as the Dutch Quarter. The neighbourhood consists of of 134 red Dutch brick buildings built from 1733 to 1740.

Saxony

The Free State of Saxony is the tenth-largest of Germany's sixteen states, situated in the east of the country. Although it is one of the smaller German federal States, it has a complex and interesting history and many historic and natural sights. Its capital is Dresden, and its largest city is Leipzig. It is a welcoming destination for a break when exploring the state or as a base for a vacation. The state is home to many historic towns and cities, such as Meissen, Freiberg, Pirna, Bautzen, and Görlitz. The sheer number of attractions, towns, villages, traditional taverns, and adorable shops is overwhelming. Just make sure to bring your camera, as the scenery is beautiful. Leipzig's active nightlife also offers something for everyone, from classical concerts to bars and discos.

Leipzig is the largest city in the state of Saxony, and the industrial center of the region. The city charms its visitors with stunning architecture, shopping possibilities, vibrant nightlife and beautiful buildings. Leipzig is a complex mixture of stunning architecture, small-town atmosphere, and scenic beauty. The composer Johann Sebastian Bach is Leipzig's most famous citizen.

Your first sightseeing stop in the city should be the Thomaskirche. The St. Thomas Church is the place where Johann Sebastian Bach worked as a precentor. His remains are buried in the church. The church is also known as the place where the reformer Martin Luther preached on Pentecost Sunday, signaling the arrival of Protestantism in the city. The Bach Museum is located right next to the church.

Leipzig's Old Town Hall is also a great place to visit. It was built in 1556 in the Renaissance style and it is one the most beautiful Renaissance structures in the country. You can't miss this imposing building as it's in a very prominent position. It is located on the main square and features the Banquetting Hall with Renaissance interior. The building also houses an interesting museum worth visiting. The Stadtgeschichtliches Museum covers the history of Leipzig. Admission cost is €2.50.

If you have kids, make sure to visit the Leipzig Zoo. It has been wow-ing visitors since 1878. The zoo covers about 225,000 square metres and contains around 850 different species. Leipzig's zoo is famous for housing the world's largest zoological facilities for primates. Kids love this experience, and for a lot of visitors, it's the highpoint of their trip. Admission cost is €17.

Don't leave Leipzig without visiting the biggest mounument in Europe. The Monument to the Battle of the Nations, also known as Völkerschlachtdenkmal, commemorates the Battle of Leipzig, and Napoleon's defeat. This beautiful structure was built in 1913 for the 100th anniversary of the battle. It is 91 metres tall and contains over 500 steps. It is located in the southeast of Leipzig.

Thuringia

Thuringia is located in the central part of the country, and is one of the smallest states in Germany. Its capital is Erfurt. Thuringia, the green heart of Germany, has a predominantly mountainous and forested terrain, but its landscapes are quite diverse. Thuringia offers plenty of activities for visitors, from riverside walks, charming villages and towns to discover, to lots of historic sites to visit. Anyone visiting the state cannot fail to appreciate the wonderful and diverse scenery and the many opportunities for outdoor activities.

Erfurt is the capital city of Thuringia. It was an important trading centre during the Middle Ages. Once you are inside the city, it is small enough to simply walk around. Erfurt makes for a great destination because it still retains a small town feel. With its narrow streets, beautiful old houses, parks and little bridges, Erfurt is much more than a quaint touristy city. It is an interesting city which retains its distinct character and the atmosphere of previous centuries.

The city has many wonderful things to offer. The streets are lined with souvenir shops, cafes, and restaurants, and the medieval city centre has numerous old timber-framed houses and beautiful churches. Probably one of the most impressive yet typical buildings in Erfurt is the Catholic Erfurt Cathedral. It is a 1200-year-old church situated on

Cathedral Hill of Erfurt. The cathedral is also known as St Mary's Cathedral. The cathedral houses rich furnishings and sculptures, including the tomb of the Count von Gleichen.

Another important tourist attraction of Erfurt is the Krämerbrücke. It is a bridge completely covered with dwellings. This beautiful city is also a haven for garden enthusiasts. If you want to picnic, take a break in Erfurts's most popular public park. The Egapark is one of the largest parks in Germany, and one of the best places for catching the sunset before dinner or a cocktail. It is the perfect place for a romantic stroll, or an afternoon picnic. You will feel like you are out of the city without having to go far.

No trip to Erfurt is complete without a visit to the Erfurt Synagogue, the oldest synagogue still standing in Europe. The building itself is used as a museum and permanently houses the Erfurt Treasure. Some parts of the Erfurt Synagogue date from the 11th century.

Saxony - Anhalt

Saxony-Anhalt is located in the central part of Germany. By size, it is the 8th largest state in the country. The state is home to several medieval cathredrals and beautiful vine-growing areas, while the

Harz mountains and beautiful old towns like Wernigerode, and Osterode are favourite tourist spots.

Magdeburg is the capital of Saxony-Anhalt and has a population of 228,800. The city used to be one of the most significant medieval cities of Europe. Today, Magdeburg has become a modern city with numerous sights, attractions, cafes, shops and restaurants. The city is situated on the Elbe River, and with so many trails and routes, Magdeburg is a paradise for anyone interested in hiking.

One of the most famous landmarks in the city is the Protestant Cathedral of Magdeburg. It is the oldest Gothic cathedral in Germany and well worth at least a short visit. It is also one of Magdeburg's most impressive buildings and one of the tallest cathedrals in eastern Germany. The cathedral is home to the grave of Emperor Otto I the Great. It is famous for its beautiful sculptures, particularly the "Twelve Virgins", and the statues of St Maurice and St Catherine.

Magdeburg's oldest building was founded in the 11th century. The Monastery of Our Lady is famous for its long and slender towers. It houses the Magdeburg Art Museum and the Georg Philipp Telemann concert hall. This is one of my favourite buildings in the city. And if all that history proves a little exhausting, head to the Gruson-Gewächshäuser. This botanical garden is one of the most popular attractions in the city. The garden was heavily damaged during the Second World War, but it was gradually restored. The garden was created by Hermann Gruson in 1895. Today the garden has 10 exhibition halls and contains more than 3000 plant species. In addition, it is one of the most peaceful places in the city.

One of Magdeburgs's architectural wonders is the Millennium Tower. It is the third highest wooden tower in the world, which is impressive. The tower was established in 1999, and houses an exhibition on the development of sciences. It has 6 floors and a spiral wooden stair. I may not be a huge fan of this kind of architecture, but the structure is one of Magdeburgs's landmarks. Make sure you don't miss this construction made of wood and bold geometric shapes. The Millennium Tower is located in the Elbauen Park. This beautiful park is a great place to spend an afternoon.

Mecklenburg-Western Pomerania

Mecklenburg-Vorpommern is the sixth largest German state. Its capital is Schwerin. The coastline of the Baltic Sea, including the Mecklenburg Lake District, features many holiday resorts and unspoilt nature, and the best way to see the area is by renting a car. Tourism is now an important industry, allowing visitors to discover the best Mecklenburg-Vorpommern has to offer. The area is a watersports haven, with more than 1,800 lakes and many rivers. Several large lakes can also be found in the area. In Mecklenburg-Vorpommern, visitors will find unspoilt beaches, and stunning landscapes. It is the ideal location for hiking and water activities.

The Baltic Coast is famous for its beautiful beaches. While you wouldn't normally relate Germany with some amazingly pristine beaches, this region located in the northern federal states of Schleswig-Holstein and Mecklenburg-Western Pomerania has something for everyone.

The Baltic Sea Coast is packed with breathtaking scenery, and picturesque panoramas, and provides the ultimate holiday experience for all. Along the coast, you will find some of the most idyllic beaches in the country. Visitors flock here each year to see the beauty of the region for themselves. The resort islands of Hiddensee and Usedom are a popular summer destination for both tourists and locals. The area offers plenty of options to keep you busy and entertained. It is one of Germany's most enchanting destinations and a good place for those who are looking for a more relaxing beach trip. As one of Germany's biggest draws when it comes to holidays, the Baltic Coast is a massive vacation hotspot, with plenty of sun and beautiful beaches.

Usedom is the second biggest island in Germany after Rügen. The largest city on the island, Świnoujście is part of the Polish West Pomeranian Voivodeship. Its scenic beauty and cultural attractions have been the stuff of legend for decades. The island is a very popular tourist destination, and has many seaside resorts including Zinnowitz, the Amber Spas in the west, and the Kaiserbad. The area is is characterized by unspoilt forests, small villages, lagoons, and hills. The island is blessed with sugar-white beaches, a number of elegant seaside towns such as Zinnowitz and Heringsdorf, and plenty of activities to try day and night.

The island lies in the delta of the Oder River. It is the sunniest area of both Germany and Poland. The island gives you the chance to experience the feel of Poland without crossing the border, and with more than 1900 sunshine hours, Usedom is also the sunniest island in the Baltic Sea. It is a delight for sun-seekers and nature lovers. The island offers a wide range of activities whether you are looking to relax or tackle the sun and surf.

This tiny piece of paradise is packed with sandy pathways, charming shops and lovely cafes. One of the top attractions on the island is the Usedom Botanical Garden. It is a private botanical garden opened in 2009. The garden contains about 50,000 plants. They are arranged by botanical classification in 14 garden areas.

The island is also home to the Karnin Lift Bridge. It is a railway bridge built in 1933. This beautiful bridge was part of the Ducherow–Swinemünde railway, and it had a total length of 360 metres. The bridge is also known as Hubbrücke Karnin. At the end of the Second World War the bridge was destroyed by the Wehrmacht, but some sections were saved.

The island also offers an extensive range of activities to keep you occupied for the duration of your stay. If you love history, or just want to learn more about it, you should visit the Dannenfeldt Mausoleum. It is a historical building, located near the 15th-century Gothic church in Mönchow. Built in 1891, the small cemetery is the final resting place of the Dannenfeldt family. You can also visit the Peenemünde Historical Technical Museum, housed in the observation bunker of the former power station. It was founded in 1991, and boasts some extraordinary exhibits, including the A4 rocket. You will need several hours to tour the museum.

When you need to escape the summer heat, head to one of the most popular holiday destinations in Germany. This is one of my favorite places in the country, so beautiful it is hard to describe. Rügen is Germany's largest island. It is located off the Pomeranian coast in the Baltic Sea, and as it's perfectly situated, you will be able to see some of the most beautiful landscapes in the country. Rügen has a length of 51.4 km, and a maximum width of 42.8 km. With its white-sand beaches, numerous lagoons, peninsulas, headlands, and open bays, Rügen has been a popular holiday destination since the 19th century. The island really does have some of the most varied and beautiful scenery in Germany, as well as seaside resorts, numerous attractions and plenty of activities to keep any visitor busy. The Jasmund National Park, a World Heritage Site is also situated here. It is famous for the largest chalk cliffs in the country.

The most popular towns on the island are Bergen, Sassnitz, Putbus and Garz. The island also has some amazing seaside resorts, such as Binz, Baabe, Göhren, Sellin and Thiessow. Bergen is the island's largest town, while Binz is the most popular and bustling beach resort. On a sunny day this beautiful island gets flooded with visitors. It is surrounded by several peninsulas and has a total area of 926.4 km^2.

For those who prefer staying dry, the island has many hidden treasures, such as the Western Pomerania Lagoon Area National Park, the Jasmund National Park, and a nature reserve, the Southeast Rügen Biosphere Reserve. The area is fast becoming one of Germany's top destinations for tourists with its large and relatively unspoiled natural environment.
The island offers a huge variety of beautiful beaches.

Swimming, surfing, and sunbathing are the favourite activities here. The area is renowned as one of the best windsurf destinations in Germany, and there are some great locations for kitesurfing around the island. This is a fascinating area to visit, with its contrasting landscapes and loads of things to do. It is so popular that it can get very crowded in summer. In addition to natural beauty, Rügen has fine sports facilities and visitor centres, so you will need plenty of energy.

The island offers numerous activities to choose from, and there is something for everyone from complete beginner to the more experienced adventurer. Numerous facilities are ideally placed to give you the adrenaline rush you crave. You can rent a bike, or you can combine the thrills of surfing and the tranquility of sailing. Just sit back, relax, and feel the wind in your hair. Go cycling, surfing or sailing. Play golf or explore the island. Riding on horseback allows you to get back to nature, and explore the island's most secluded beaches and beautiful surroundings. We should not forget to mention the experience of flying in a hot air balloon over the beautiful island. Several agencies provide scenic hot air balloon rides. There are so many available options that you might not know where to begin.

A portrait of Northern Germany: Schleswig - Holstein

Schleswig-Holstein is the northernmost state of Germany. The state is one of the flattest parts of the country, while the Baltic Sea coast is dominated by bays and fjords. The state is a great place for walkers with its quiet trails and attractive landscape. Bordered by the North Sea and the Baltic Sea, the state is very popular with outdoor enthusiasts for the range of activities it offers.

Kiel is the capital and most populous city located at the Baltic Sea in the state of Schleswig-Holstein. The city is dotted with many interesting and historic sites worth seeing. Kiel is a charming city with numerous attractions and a number of annual festivals. There are lots of bars with traditional and other styles of music, as well as nightclubs, and many restaurants. Kiel is a manageable, walkable city with great vibe and amazing views.

The city is also an important sea transport hub and a great destination for anyone interested in outdoor activities, such as walking, hiking, sailing, or watersports. Due to its geographic location, the city is famous for its international sailing events, including the annual Kiel Week. The Kiel Week s the world's biggest sailing event and one of Germany's largest festivals. The Kiel Week is held annually in the last complete week in June.

During the Second World War, Kiel was heavily bombed, and the bombing destroyed almost all historic landmarks in the city. However, one of the most interesting places in the city is the Laboe Naval Memorial, also known as the Laboe Tower. It is dedicated to the sailors of all nationalities who died during the World Wars. Laboe is also home to the World War II submarine U 995.

The city also has two botanical gardens, the Old Botanical Garden and New Botanical Garden. The Old Botanical Garden contains more than 280 species of diverse herbaceous flora, two ponds, lawn areas, and an interesting collection of trees. The New Botanical Garden features several greenhouses and contains 14,000 plant species. The garden also include an arboretum with tree collections and a pond.

Kiel also features a number of museums, including geological, historical, industrial, and military museums. The city is located close to the sea, so the beaches such as Strande, Kiel Schilksee, and Laboe are also extremely popular places to visit.

Hamburg

The second largest city in Germany, Hamburg is a major transport hub and a melting pot of architecture, tourism, and culture and an important financial centre. Hamburg is the ninth largest city in the European Union and home to the second largest port in Europe. Hamburg literally has something for everyone. Whether you are a person who likes to shop, dance, hike or just experience the culture you will find that here. Strolling the streets of Hamburg is like journeying back in time. The Old Town is Hamburg's oldest district and the real attraction for visitors. The city has more bridges than any other city in the world and more canals and streams than Amsterdam and Venice combined. And this is just the beginning.

One of the most famous landmarks in the city, the Gothic Revival Church of St. Nicholas was the world's tallest building in the 19th century. This church was one of the five Lutheran churches in the city. Unfortunately, the church is almost completely ruined, but it is still an important architectural landmark. The church was bombed during the second world war, and it is still one of the tallest structures in the city.

Hamburg is proud of its rich heritage, historically significant events, vibrant nightlife and popular landmarks. The city boasts more than 40 theatres, 60 museums and 100 clubs. Hamburg has several large world renowned museums and galleries worth visiting, such as the Hamburg Kunsthalle and the Archäologisches Museum Hamburg. The Deutsches Schauspielhaus, the Thalia Theatre, and the Kampnagel are some of the most popular theatres in the city.

The Chilehaus is one of several hidden gems located in the Kontorhausviertel. This iconic building is an amazing example of the famous Brick Expressionism style of architecture. It was built between 1922 and 1924, and looks like a giant shiny ship. This beautiful structure is among the most architecturally impressive buildings in the city. If you want to see something really spectacular, head to Miniatur Wunderland. It is the world's largest model railway exhibition. The interactive exhibit is spread out over 6,400 square meters and is divided into seven sections: Harz, the Alps and Austria, Hamburg, America, Scandinavia, and Switzerland. The city's most popular destination has attracted more than 10 million visitors since it opened. The inner child in you will surely jump out once you see it.

If you are a photographer or nature lover, this is definitely the place to go.
Planten un Blomen is an urban park and an oasis in the city providing an escape from the hustle and bustle of city life. It was established in 1930. The park is famed for its water-light concerts, various events and music

performances. There is also a large playground in the southern area of the park. The park is open all year round and there is no entrance fee. The Old Botanical Garden of Hamburg is situated within the park.

Hamburg has a fascinating mix of museums, galleries, atrractions and parks. The Internationales Maritimes Museum is one of the best museums in the city. It is a private museum located in the HafenCity quarter. Even if you are not a big fan of museums, the building itself is worth a visit for its beautiful architecture. This interesting museum is housed in a former warehouse. The museum contains Peter Tamm's collection of model ships, construction plans, uniforms, and maritime art. It also has more than one million photographs.

This is one of the best cities in the country when it comes to shopping. Hamburg is a world-renowned shopping, dining and entertainment destination. From quaint boutiques, traditional shops to expansive shopping malls, Hamburg has it all. The main shopping area is located in the center of the city around the Binnenalster, and the Europa Passage is a must-see shopping destination while visiting Hamburg. It is one of the largest shopping malls in Hamburg. The mall has 120 stores on five floors, and a large selection of food courts.

Another place worth visiting is the Neuer Wall. It is a busy shopping district located near the Mönckebergstraße. The street is lined with luxury brands and it is by far the trendiest place to shop in Hamburg. In fact, the Neuer Wall is one of the most exclusive shopping streets in Europe. For the budget-minded, head to the Mönkebergstraße. It is the oldest traditional shopping district in the city. The area is home to several departments stores, traditional shops, and various retail stores.

Bremen

Bremen is a commercial and industrial city and the third most populous city in Northern Germany. It is also one of the 3 city states in Germany. Bremen consists of two enclaves, Bremen and Bremerhaven. Located on the river Weser, Bremen has a very long history. The city was an important member of the medieval Hanseatic League and is still one of the most important cities in the country.

The city has a major port on the River Weser. There is also a huge choice of accommodations, places to eat, and plenty of entertainment of all kinds. It makes a great base for anyone exploring the country. The world famous Beck's Beer is brewed in Bremen. The entire area is blessed with a huge choice for anyone interested in history. The Bremen City Hall is one of the most famous landmarks in the city. It is the seat of the President of the Senate and Mayor of the city of Bremen. In addition, the building is one of the best examples of Brick Gothic architecture in Europe. Located in the historic city centre, this beautiful structure was inscribed on the list of UNESCO World Heritage Sites, together with the Roland of Bremen. The Bremen Roland is a statue of Roland, paladin of the first Holy Roman Emperor Charlemagne. The New Town Hall is adjacent to the older section of the Town Hall. The hall on a bright sunny day is one of Bremen's must-see sights.

Another fascinating place to visit is the famous Bremen Cathedral, dedicated to St. Peter. The cathedral is situated in the market square, in the historic city centre.

Photo by Dirk Duckhorn licensed under CC BY-SA 2.0 via Flickr

The Am Wall Windmill is well worth at least a short visit. It is an important and iconic building and a lovely park which offers a place to sit and relax. The first windmill was constructed in 1699. Today, this structure is open to visitors and features a lovely restaurant.

In addition to historic buildings, Bremen has a lot of interesting museums. If more contemporary activities interest you, head to the Universum Bremen. It is a science museum and boasts approximately 250 exhibits. This innovative museum invites visitors to discover the fascinating world of science. A visit is a great experience for the whole family, but especially for kids. Admission costs €16.00 per person.

Lower Saxony

Lower Saxony is situated in northwestern Germany. It is a great destination for anyone interested in hiking, with plenty of different facilities for visitors. The state capital is Hanover. Lower Saxony is a very fertile country, dominated by several rivers. Agriculture remains one of the most important sectors in the economy.

Hanover is the capital of Lower Saxony. The city is situated on the River Leine, and is located 285 km west of Berlin. Hanover is also the country's thirteenth largest city, and hosts annual trade fairs such as the Hanover Fair and the CeBIT. The city is also home to the Oktoberfest Hannover, the second largest Oktoberfest in the world. Hanover is a pleasant city, with interesting shops and plenty of cafes, bars and restaurants. It is also a cultural city with many theaters, cinemas, galleries and museums, as well as many interesting attractions worth seeing. However, the city has only a few historical landmarks. Hanover was an important road junction with its industrial sites, and a major target for bombing during World War II. The city center was almost completely destroyed and devastated.

You will find it hard not to notice the world-famous baroque gardens. The Royal Gardens of Herrenhausen were created in the 17th century to copy the Versailles Garden in France. They are a heritage of the Kings of Hanover and are made up of the Great Garden, the Berggarten, the Georgengarten and the Welfengarten. This is a popular place to visit especially during the summer time. The Great Garden of Herrenhausen is particularly beautiful. Every summer, the garden hosts a large variety of festivals and other theatrical performances.

The Great Garden consists of several parts and includes a large number of hedges, walkways, and statues, as well as the Great Ground and the Nouveau Jardin. Unfortunately, the Herrenhausen Castle, was largely destroyed by Allied bombing during World War II.

The Berggarten is also worth exploring. It was created in 1666, and includes the Tropical House, the Cactus House, the Canary House and the Orchid House. There are also the historic Library Pavillon and the Mausoleum of the Guelphs. It is a lovely area for walking, or just relaxing in attractive surroundings.

Near the Berggarten entrance, there is also an impressive Sea Life Centre well worth visiting. The Georgengarten and the Welfengarten are the landscape gardens, and the Georgenpalais houses the Wilhelm Busch Museum. The gardens make a great setting for a picnic or stroll. If that is not enough to keep you and your kids busy, head to the Hanover Zoo. It is one of the best zoos in Europe. The zoo consists of several theme areas, and has a tropical house, a jungle house, and a show arena. Admission costs €25 for adults.

If you are in the area, you shouldn't miss the Marienburg Castle, located in the municipality of Pattensen. It is a Gothic revival castle built between 1858 and 1867. You can embark on a history tour that will take you back to the 19th century. Highlights are the castle museum, the restaurant, and the chapel. The area's unspoiled environment makes it an ideal destination for walking. Admission costs €7 for adults. Some other popular sights in the city are the Old Town and the Marktkirche, as well as the Luther Church, and the Gehry Tower.

A portrait of Western Germany: North Rhine Westphalia

North Rhine-Westphalia is Germany's most populous state. The state capital is Düsseldorf, and the biggest city is Cologne. Some of the largest cities in Germany, such as Cologne, Dortmund, and Essen are also located in North Rhine-Westphalia. Düsseldorf lies at the centre of the Lower Rhine basin and it is the seventh most populous city in the country, with a population of almost 600,000. The city is also an international business and financial centre. It was heavily destroyed in the Second World War. However, Düsseldorf's various attractions and activities cater to just about every age and interest, and the bustling city center is compact enough to explore on foot. The city is packed with unique boutiques, shops, art galleries and dozens of excellent restaurants. And there are plenty of things to do, especially for the younger crowd. Most things in Düsseldorf have an artistic flair. The city's main attractions, popular landmarks, shopping districts and nightlife venues are all clustered within walking distance of one another. Düsseldorf has numerous museums, shopping districts and nightclubs that provide plenty of entertainment.

Düsseldorf isn't just a big city, it is much more than that. It is a year-round destination, with plenty to do in every season. To get a glimpse of Düsseldorf from a different angle, head to the Rheinturm. It is a 240.5 metre high telecommunications tower and houses a lovely revolving restaurant and an observation deck. The observation deck is open daily from 10:00 am to 11:30 pm. Located near the Media Harbor, the

Rheinturm also features the largest digital clock in the world.

The best way to get a feel for the area is to simply stroll down its main streets. Stadtmitte is an urban borough perfect for strolling around. The Königsallee is also worth exploring. It is an urban boulevard and one of the city's main arteries. In addition to fashionable shops, there are art galleries, antique shops and bookstores filled with lovely books and treasures.

To get a taste of this bustling metropolis, head to the Benrather Schloss. It is a Baroque palace surrounded by a lovely park. This charming structure was built for the Elector Palatine and Duke of Bavaria Charl Theodor and his beloved wife Countess Elisabeth Auguste of Sulzbach. Construction began in 1755, and this palace is considered to be one of the most beautiful palaces of the Rococo epoch. There is also a museum with guided tours.

Another must-see is the Wilhelm Marx House. It is located in the central district of Düsseldorf and it was Germany's first high-rise building. The building was built in 1924 and it was also one of the first skyscrapers in Europe. The structure is 57 meters high and has 13 floors. It also features a theatre.

Cologne is Germany's fourth-largest city and the largest city both in the German Federal State of North Rhine-Westphalia and within the Rhine-Ruhr

Metropolitan Area. Situated on the river Rhine, Cologne is one of the most liberal cities in the country. Whether you have a few hours or a few days, you will love the look and charm of this lovely city. Cologne is full of museums, restaurants and many other places to visit, so you won't be lacking of things to do. The architecture, sights and flavours of the city are quite impressive and will leave you in awe. One of the top tourist attractions in Cologne is definitely Kölner Dom. The Dom is the largest cathedral in Germany and the seat of the Archbishop of Cologne. It is also Germany's most visited landmark and a UNESCO World Heritage Site. Entry into the cathedral is free.

The city is a great place to go if you are looking to learn more about our history and culture. Don't forget to visit the twelve beautifully preserved Romanesque churches of Cologne located in the Old town of Cologne. Cologne is a modern and vibrant city, but it is famous for its traditional neighborhoods. The bohemian Agnesviertel is one of Cologne's most beloved neighborhoods. It is packed with trendy stores, bookshops, bars, and art galleries. You can also explore some historical structures, such as the North City Gate.

You can really see the diversity of Cologne at night, so make sure to stop by the Hohenzollern Bridge. The bridge crosses the Rhine and it was constructed between 1907 and 1911. The total length of the bridge is 409.19 meters. And when it comes to nightlife in Cologne, the city is home to a vibrant nightlife scene. Depending on your tastes, you can find classical concerts, bars, discos, or just a good place to relax with a glass of wine or a beer.

Rhineland-Palatinate

Rhineland-Palatinate has everything from a famously scenic section of the Rhine to blue crater lakes. Located in western Germany, it is the largest wine producing area in the country. The city of Mainz is the state capital. The largest river in the state is the Rhine. Mainz is located on the river Rhine and it is well known for its Roman heritage. Once the seat of the Electorate of Mainz, the city is an attractive place to explore. It also has a great range of shops, restaurants and bars. The city bustles with life, and attracts visitors interested in history, architecture and culture. Visitors can spend their spare time in the city enjoying the boutique shops and tasty restaurants.

The most popular attractions in Mainz include an impressive Roman remains, several renowned museums and beautiful buildings. Mainz retains a charming, rather old-fashioned feeling, with its colorful houses and buildings. Among the most fascinating buildings in the city is the Iron Tower, a medieval tower built in the 13th century. This imposing structure served as a watchtower and later as a prison.

The building itself was heavily damaged in World War II and reconstructed in the 1960s. Today it houses various events and is msotly used for art exhibitions.

Anyone interested in learning something of Germany's history will enjoy a visit to the historical center and pedestrianized market square of Mainz. Nearby is the cathedral of St. Martin, which has become a symbol of the city. It is one of the oldest cathedrals in Germany, and the site of the episcopal see of the Bishop of Mainz. The cathedral houses tombs of former Electoral-prince-archbishops. Before leaving Mainz, take the time to visit the **Theodor Heuss Bridge**, which connects the Mainz-Kastel district of Wiesbaden, the state of Hesse and Mainz. The bridge was built by the Romans in 27 AD. Unfortunately, it was completely destroyed at the end of the Second World War. This imposing bridge was rebuilt in the early 1950s and named after the first president of the Federal Republic of Germany, Theodor Heuss.

Hesse

Hesse is both a cultural region and the name of an individual state. The State of Hesse is smaller than the cultural region of Hesse, and it is situated in west-central Germany. Its capital is Wiesbaden, while Frankfurt is the largest city of Hesse. With dramatic peaks, beautiful rivers and pristine lakes, the state is an outdoor enthusiast's paradise. Hesse is the greenest state in the country, and with so much unspoiled natural beauty, make some time to soak in the scenery. With verdant mountains, and hiking trails that stretch for miles, there is plenty to excite adventure lovers in this area.

Frankfurt is the largest city in the state of Hesse in the south-western part of Germany, and the fifth-largest city in the country. It is also one of the most well-known cities in Germany. The city constantly ranks among the world's leading financial centres, but it is much more than that. There are many things to do in Frankfurt including everything from shopping to sightseeing. Frankfurt is also a major centre for business, commerce, culture, education, and tourism. With such diversity to experience, the city is both an urban and a natural playground. Located on the river Main, Frankfurt is famous for its futuristic appearance, but the city also offers a variety of other attractions like museums, shops and restaurants.

The best place to begin discovering Frankfurt is certainly the Römerberg. The Römerberg is the historic heart of Frankfurt, and the old centre of the city. I will never get tired of coming here over and over again. The area has a number of historic buildings dating to the 14th and 15th century, including the city hall.

A lively place full of people, Paulsplatz is a historic square in the heart of the city. It is the largest square in the old town. St Paul's Church is located here. The church was built between 1789 and 1833, and the building was once the seat of the first democratically elected Parliament. Like most historic buildings in Germany, it was destroyed during World War II, and then rebuilt. The building is no longer used as a church. Today the building is used as a venue used for various events.

Saint Bartholomeus' Cathedral is a Roman Catholic Gothic church dedicated to Saint Bartholomew. It is one of the city's major draws for locals and tourists. Constructed in the 14th century, the cathedral was an imperial collegiate church, built on the foundation of an earlier church. The height of the structure is 95

metres. If you are not up for strolling, visit some of Frankfurt's beloved outdoor attractions like the Eiserner Steg. Built in 1869, it is a pedestrian-only bridge which connects the Römerberg and Sachsenhausen. The bridge is also one of the symbols of this wonderful city.

Many museums in the city are located in a district called Museumsufer. If you like museums, then you should head to the German Architecture Museum. The museum is housed in an 18th-century building and has a collection of architectural drawings and models, and a reference library. Admission is €6.00 for adults.

Frankfurt is one of the world's most fashionable cities with endless stores to explore. There are several areas in Frankfurt that are worth a visit if you are planning a shopping trip. Some are located in central Frankfurt, while others are a bit more off the beaten track. Your first stop should be the Zeil. The Zeil is Frankfurt's main shopping district and one of the most popular and busiest shopping streets in Germany. The area is full of well-known department stores, retail chains and specialty shops. There are also numerous small shops and boutiques with clothes, shoes, leather goods, and jewellery.

If you've got deep pockets, head to Goethestraße. It is a luxury shopping street located between Opernplatz and Börsenstraße. The street is lined with many designer boutiques and exclusive department stores

Frankfurt's city centre offers plenty of opportunities for shopping. In the same area is Schillerstrasse, where you can find numerous gift shops and specialist shops. And if you are looking for some hard-to-find items, and second-hand outlets, head to Berger Straße. The area is fantastic for shopping and exploring the western part of Frankfurt. Aside from numerous shops and restaurants, this mall is also home to a large spa. Located right next to the Frankfurt Fair, the mall has over 180 stores including H&M, Zara, Desigual and Pull&Bear.

Saarland

Saarland is Germany's smallest federal state. Its capital is Saarbrücken, and despite its size, Saarland offers a great choice of activities and great traditional hospitality in its many pubs, restaurants and taverns. The state is named after the Saar River. Located in the west of the country, this beautiful state is generally mountainous.

Saarbrücken is the capital of Saarland and its administrative, commercial and cultural centre. The city is a good place to stop and take a walk or even stay. Saarbrücken is attractive, full of life, with lots of traditional shops, cafes, and places to eat. The city is also dotted with many interesting and historic buildings and structures, such as the stone bridge across the Saar and the Gothic church of St Arnual. Before doing anything else, take a walk along the walls of the medieval city, and visit the St. Johanner Markt. The picturesque alleys and streets are scattered around the market square. The area has a lot of boutiques, bars, cafes and restaurants.

If you are in the city, you shouldn't miss one of the most famous castles in the state. The Saarbrücken Castle is a Baroque castle located in the district of Alt-Saarbrücken on the left bank of the river Saar. The castle was destroyed several times before being magnificently renovated in 1989. Built in 1575, this château is now both an administrative centre and a venue for various cultural events. Admission is free.

The St. Arnual is one of the oldest parts of the city. The 13th century Gothic church is amongst the most important historical monuments in the area. The church houses the tombs of the counts of Nassau-Saarbrücken.

A portrait of Southern Germany: Bavaria

Bavaria is Germany's largest state and the favored holiday destination of both locals and tourists. It is located in the southeast of Germany. Munich, Bavaria's capital and largest city, is the third largest city in the country. Bavaria shares borders with Austria and the Czech Republic as well as with Switzerland. The biggest cities in this state are Munich, Nuremberg, Augsburg, Regensburg, Würzburg, Ingolstadt, and Erlangen. Bavaria is home to 12.5 million inhabitants.

Many historic towns in Bavaria have retained their charm, offering visitors a unique visual and culinary experience. From a wealth of cultural treasures, ornamental baroque churches, warm hospitality, medieval towns and picturesque villages, to crystal-clear lakes and beautiful forests, Bavaria has it all. The Free State of Bavaria with its medieval castles, sparkling lakes, national parks, and magnificent palaces is a paradise for nature and wildlife lovers as well as food and wine conoisseurs.

The Romantic Road, the Castle Route, the German Alpine Road and many other popular scenic routes are perfect for exploring the region's finest landscapes. The Free State of Bavaria has more than 100,000 monuments, around 1,200 museums, and numerous world-class restaurants.

Munich is the capital and largest city of the German state of Bavaria, and the third largest city in Germany, after Berlin and Hamburg. Situated on the banks of River Isar north of the Bavarian Alps, Munich is a major finance centre and one of the most prosperous cities in Germany. Munich is home to numerous architectural attractions, famous sports events, major universities, museums and theaters.

If you are visiting Munich for the first time, finding your way around the city by foot can be complicated. However, getting lost in the narrow streets is a quintessential part of exploring Munich, and at some point you will surely end up in Marienplatz. It is a central square in the city centre of Munich. It is a vibrant, lively area full of some of the best things Munich has to offer. The city's main square is home to the Mariensäule, the Marian Column crowned with a statue of the Virgin Mary, erected in 1638.

While you are here, you should definitely visit the Englischer Garten. It is one of the world's largest public parks. It is larger than New York's Central Park, and the perfect place for a romantic stroll, or an afternoon picnic. Additionally, the park offers many leisure activities and programs throughout the year. You can rent a paddle boat, stroll along the paths, or visit one of its traditional beer gardens. The choice is up to you.

History buffs will want to visit the Munich Residence. It is the former royal palace of the Bavarian monarchs. Located at the edge of Munich's old town this palace is the largest palace in the country. It is a very large building and has an amazing collection of a wide variety of items used by royals. Many major attractions and popular landmarks are located within walking distance of one another.

The Cathedral of Our Dear Lady is the largest church in Munich. Known simply as the Frauenkirche, this church is a symbol of the Bavarian capital city. Located in Munich's old quarter, this imposing twin-towered cathedral was built in 1494. Its sturdy domed towers were added in 1525. Built in the late Gothic style, this church has a simple, yet striking layout.

Munich is also known as a premier shopping destination. The city is filled with great shopping options including some pretty amazing boutiques, so you will definitely find something that will fit your interests. Every big-name designer you can think of has a store in Munich. Several shopping centres and department

stores offer a good selection of clothing. Your first stop should be the Olympia Einkaufszentrum. It is Munich's largest shopping mall where you will find shops with some of the best items Munich has to offer. There are also a number of restaurants and cafes.

If you are looking for something unique check out the Maximilianstraße boulevard. It is one of the most exclusive and posh areas in the city. Here you can find some internationally renowned luxury shops and exclusive designer boutiques. Munich has no shortage of fantastic shopping malls. The Fünf Höfe is a beautiful mall located directly in the center of the city. The mall earned a reputation for having several trendy and international stores like Armani, Zara, Dolce & Gabbana, and Marc O'Polo. From boutiques to an upscale shops, some of Munich's best shopping can be found in this area.

Baden-Württemberg

Baden-Württemberg is Germany's third largest state. The state capital and largest city is Stuttgart. Baden-Württemberg shares borders with France, Switzerland, Rhineland Palatinate, Hessen and Bavaria. Home to the world famous Black Forest, Baden-Württemberg is one of the best tourist destinations in Germany.

Stuttgart is the sixth-largest city in the country, as well as the capital of the state of Baden-Württemberg. The city was founded in the 10th century and boasts a rich history. You will find some stunning examples of architecture dating right back to the 10th century.

Numerous things to do in Stuttgart will surprise you as Stuttgart is one of the most diverse cities in the country. The narrow streets are oozing with charm and are well worth exploring. Stuttgart also offers plenty of cultural attractions, including museums and outdoor markets. The city is nestled between hills, valley and vineyards, and it lies about an hour from the Black Forest. Stuttgart is also a centre of mechanical and automobile engineering, and home of major industries, including Mercedes-Benz and Porsche.

A great way to start your exploration of Stuttgart is to visit the Old Castle located in the centre of the city. This magnificent castle is commonly known as Altes Schloss and dates back to the 10th century. Today this castle houses the Württemberg State Museum. The Old Castle stands right next to the New Palace, which was built in the 18th century. The New Palace is located on the south edge of Schlossplatz, the central square in Stuttgart. This imposing palace served as a residence of the kings of Württemberg and it was almost completely destroyed in World War II. Currently, the building is used by the State Ministries of Finance and Education.

One of the most famous sights in the city is the Ludwigsburg Palace. It is a historical palace located in the city of Ludwigsburg. This imposing palace is one of the country's biggest Baroque palaces and features a large garden. In the 18th century the palace served as the main royal palace of the dukedom.

Once you have explored all of the above attractions, head to the Castle Solitude. It was built as a hunting lodge and summer residence of Duke Karl Eugen of Württemberg. It is located on a high plain outside Stuttgart and offers views over Weilimdorf, Korntal and Ludwigsburg. Built in 1769, the castle looks like a rococo palace.

If you feel the need to escape to wide, green spaces visit the Green U. It is a lovely spot for a bit of relaxation. Basically, the Green U is a series of parks and gardens located around the city centre. This oasis starts at the Schlossgarten, continuing through Rosensteinpark and ending in Killesberg Park.

There are also many fun activities for kids. For a laid-back, colourful ambiance, visit the Wilhelma zoo. It was built as a royal palace, and today is a zoo and botanical garden. The zoo is home to over 8,000 animals and more than 5,000 species of plants. The zoo is located in the northern suburbs of the city, but it can be easily accessed by car or tram.

The Rosensteinpark borders Stuttgart's Wilhelma zoo. Passing through the area, you will see numerous gardens, fountains and vineyards. The area offers numerous opportunities to enjoy a thousand and one activities. You can also visit the Max-Eyth-See. It is a large lake and an official nature reserve, surrounded by an expansive open area.

If you are a car enthusiast, you've probably heard of the Mercedes-Benz Museum. And if you haven't, it is an automobile museum which covers the history of the Mercedes-Benz brand. The museum is located near the Daimler factory and contains more than 160 vehicles.

If you are looking for ideas on how to spend your leisure time, this phenomenal city has plenty on offer. In Stuttgart you will find shopping surprises around every corner. The city is known for its superior selection of shops and boutiques. The Königstrasse is the city's main shopping street and one of the most popular areas in Stuttgart. The street is lined with numerous shops, department stores, cafes, restaurants and relaxation areas. The Bohnenviertel is also a wonderful place to stroll around. This is a lively area where you can find various bookstores, antique shops, galleries, jewellery and craft shops. Along Calwer

Strasse you can find some luxury shops and elegant boutiques.

While Stuttgart has some great outdoor shopping areas, there are still many indoor malls worth visiting. The Koenigsbau Passage is a large inner-city mall with more than 70 stores and restaurants on five levels.

Chapter 11: Where to stay - Best hotels and hostels

As one would expect, Germany boasts a great number of accommodation options varying from modest hostels to luxurious hotels. And each hotel has its own style and atmosphere. Since every person has different needs, you will need to ask yourself what is most important to you. Generally speaking, price is the main determining factor, and prices vary according to the type of accommodation. Choosing a hotel that is centrally located is probably your best bet, so you don't waste hours of your precious vacation time wandering around. In general, you can't go wrong with the hotels mentioned below. Each is centrally located and personally selected. All of these hotels are ideal for both business and leisure travelers. With convenient locations, these hotels also offer wonderful amenities and a range of options to suit every budget. Needless to say, it is important to remember to closely examine each hotel before placing your reservations.

Berlin

The choice of accommodations in Berlin is extensive. The city is home to a wide array of high-end hotels, and each hotel is more beautiful and unique than the next. But choosing accommodations in Berlin can be a daunting experience. There are literally hundreds of hotels in dozens of neighborhoods. Some of the best hotels in the city are within walking distance of many major attractions, as well as shopping, dining and entertainment.

One of the most fascinating hotels in Berlin is definitely the Radisson Blu Hotel. It is a luxury 5-star hotel, and a relaxing place to stay. It is close to all the city's attractions, yet peaceful. The hotel has an original look and features the world's largest cylindrical aquarium. The hotel also has a superb restaurant, an indoor pool and a stunning spa for those who feel the need to unwind after a long day of sightseeing. Free WiFi is also available. The Radisson Blu Hotel is located in the historic Mitte neighborhood, so you are in the middle of everything the old historic area has to offer.
(Address: Karl-Liebknecht-Straße 3, 10178 Berlin)

The Hotel Indigo Berlin – Alexanderplatz is a 4 star hotel located in the district of Mitte. The hotel offers the best of contemporary amenities in a beautiful setting. The hotel has a restaurant, a fitness center, and a bar. In addition, the hotel also features a business center, and meeting rooms.
(Address: Bernhard-Weiss-Str. 5 Berlin BE 10178)

The Circus Berlin Hotel is a 3 star hotel opened in 2008, by the owners of the famous Circus Hostel in Berlin. It is the perfect hotel for young travellers and offers good value for the money. It is located on the northern edge of Mitte, Berlin's central district. The Circus combines a fantastic location with comfortable accommodations. The hotel features a bar, a 24-hour front desk, and a computer station. (Address: Rosenthaler Str. 1, 10119 Berlin).

Munich

There is a huge choice of accommodations in Munich. Many of the hotels are within walking distance or close to public transportation and major attractions. Housed in a 19th-century building, the Sofitel Munich Bayerpost is a welcome oasis located in the heart of the city. This hotel is situated only a few steps from Munich's main train station and offers an indoor pool, and spacious rooms. Make the most of your trip, by taking some time to relax as you will also find a sauna on offer. It is an ideal destination for business travel or a special getaway.(Address: Bayerstraße 12, 80335 München)

The Platz Hotel is a 4 star hotel located in Altstadt-Lehel. It is within a 5-minute walk of Hofbrauhaus and Marienplatz. The hotel features a health club, a bar, a

steam room, and a sauna. With its prime location, the Platz Hotel puts you steps from Munich's famous sights.
(Address: Sparkassenstraße 10, 80331 München)

If you are really tight on cash, consider staying in a hostel. Opened in 2004, the Wombat´s City Hostel is really a home away from home. It is a great place to stay while you explore Munich and the local area. This charming hostel is located right next to Hauptbahnhof, and offers everything from 8 bed dorms to private doubles with ensuite bathrooms. It also **puts you within easy reach of all the attractions in the city.** (Address: Senefelderstraße 1, 80336 München).

Hamburg

Hamburg is home to many of the nation's largest hotels. Many hotels also have free shuttles for guests, and jaw-dropping views. If you want to be in the middle of all that Hamburg has to offer, then look no further. The Park Hyatt Hamburg is a 5 star hotel, and offers a full-service spa, several restaurants and an indoor pool. Other amenities include a health club and a lovely bar. The Park Hyatt Hamburg is located steps away from the Mönckebergstraße, one of the main shopping streets in the city. (Address: Bugenhagenstraße 8, 20095 Hamburg)

The Madison Hotel is a stylish 4 star hotel located in central Hamburg, just near the St. Michaelis Church. The hotel sits within blocks of the city's best attractions and restaurants. The hotel features a full-service spa, a restaurant and an indoor pool. There is also a health club, a fitness center, and a bar. (Address: Schaarsteinweg 4, 20459 Hamburg)

If you are on a budget, I would recommend to check out the Generator Hostel Hamburg. It offers a bar, a coffee shop and laundry facilities. This lovely hostel boasts a lively atmosphere for you to enjoy whilst exploring the city. (Address: Steintorpl. 3, 20099 Hamburg).

Stuttgart

Whatever you and your family are looking for, Stuttgart has what you may need. Le Méridien Stuttgart is one of the most elegant hotels in the city. The hotel features a full-service spa, an indoor pool, 2 restaurants, a health club, a bar, and a sauna. This luxury hotel is conviniently located in the green heart of Stuttgart, near the beautiful gardens of Schlossgarten Park. Enchanting experiences await every guest who visits this wonderful hotel. (Address: Willy-Brandt-Straße 30, 70173 Stuttgart)

The Pullman Fontana Hotel lies in Stuttgart's Vaihingen district. The hotel offers business and leisure amenities that are sure to please even the most discerning guests. Along with a full-service spa, this luxury hotel has a restaurant, a fitness center, a bar, an indoor pool, and a poolside bar.
(Address: Vollmoellerstrasse 5, 70563 Stuttgart-Vaihingen).

A charming hostel, Alex 30 is conveniently located in the center of the city, but kilometres away from an ordinary experience. Its location makes it an excellent place to stay. The hostel features an internet café, Wi-Fi and a terrace with barbecue area. This hostel combines a friendly service and the comforts of home all in one place. (Address: Alexanderstraße 30, 70184 Stuttgart).

Frankfurt

Choosing the right hotel is about finding the hotel that suits your needs. But there is so much diversity in Frankfurt, it can be difficult to know where to start.

The Westin Grand Hotel is the perfect base to explore Frankfurt. Located in the heart of Frankfurt, this luxury hotel offers 3 restaurants, a lobby lounge, an Executive Club Lounge, and a 24-hour WestinWORKOUT® center. In addition, it also features an indoor pool and a full service spa. (Address: Konrad-Adenauer-Straße 7, 60313 Frankfurt am Main)

The Concorde Hotel is a 4 star hotel located in Bahnhofsviertel. Housed in a restored century-old building, it is an inviting hotel where business and vacation travelers can relax. The hotel features a bar, a business center, and self parking. WiFi in public areas is free.
(Address: Karlstraße 9, 60329 Frankfurt am Main)

In case you want to immerse yourself in traditional German culture, then look no further. The Five Elements Hostel is close to the Städel, and Frankfurt Opera House. It has a great central location, and is surrounded by a rich culture just waiting to be discovered. This quirky hostel promises a fun and comfortable atmoshphere. It offers a bar, a 24-hour front desk, free newspapers, and laundry facilities.
(Address: Moselstraße 40, 60329 Frankfurt am Main)

Chapter 12: Amazing small towns in Germany and popular travel destinations

It's no secret that Germany boasts some of the world's most gorgeous regions and towns and has some strikingly diverse landscapes. In fact, the country is dotted with a sizable number of beautiful historic towns where you can explore many attractions without the stress of busy cities. As a general rule, many travelers base themselves in Berlin or Munich, but the rest of the country should not be missed. If you are more interested in discovering the country's natural wonders, you will find plenty of places to do so. Many of the towns have well-preserved medieval areas and numerous sights and attractions.

Lübeck

Of all the smaller towns in Schleswig-Holstein, in northern Germany, Lübeck is arguably the most interesting and most beautiful. The city is perfect for all kinds of activities, from walking, and cycling, to picnicking or simply meeting up with friends. Only a short, scenic drive from Hamburg, this beautiful, charming, and good-natured town offers more than enough to keep you busy for a couple of days. Situated on the river Trave, the city is also one of the major ports of Germany. Much of the old town has preserved a medieval appearance with beautiful old buildings and narrow streets.

During the cold weather, you can explore one of the top-notch museums in the city. The St. Anne's Museum is located near St. Giles Church in the south-east of the city. This museum boasts a few special features that set it apart from Lübeck's other beloved museums. The museum houses an impressive collection of medieval sculpture and altar-pieces, and a large collection of home decor items. In addition, the St. Anne's Museum is part of the Lübeck World Heritage site.

Known for its architectural wonders, medieval buildings, and excellent restaurants, Lübeck is one of the most magical cities in the country. Surrounded by water, the old town is mainly composed of seven Gothic-style church towers. The churches contains some of the finest Northern German artworks. Most notable church is the Lübecker Dom. It is a large brick-built cathedral that still dominates the old town centre. Founded in 1173, the Lübecker Dom is the oldest cathedral in the city. Known as the City of Seven Spires, Lübeck has many wonderful churches to explore.

The city's most prominent landmark is the well known Holstentor, which is one of two remaining city gates.

Built in 1464, it is often regarded as a symbol of Lübeck. This Brick Gothic construction has been a UNESCO World Heritage Site since 1987. The best way to get around the city is on foot. And if you do get tired of sightseeing, the streets are lined with superb restaurants, small shops, and delightful boutiques. Lübeck truly makes a rewarding daytrip from Hamburg, but few would regret staying longer. By train, you can easily reach Lübeck from anywhere in the country.

Nuremberg

Germany is well known for its small cities and picturesque villages, and one of the most beautiful cities is definitely Nuremberg. The city is situated on the Pegnitz river and the Rhine–Main–Danube Canal in the state of Bavaria. Nuremberg is the second largest city in Bavaria, and Franconia's largest city, but it manages to give the impression of a small village. Located about 170 kilometers north of Munich, Nuremberg is the economic, social and cultural center of Franconia. The city overflows with jaw-dropping architecture, gothic churches, romantic corners, trendy boutiques, fantastic restaurants and renowned museums. Nuremberg is chock full of attractions for every interest and budget. In addition, Nuremberg hosts dozens of festivals throughout the year.

This eminently walkable city has a unique feel. Among the many interesting places to visit is the Nuremberg Castle, situated in the north-western corner of Nuremberg's old town. The area includes three sections; the Imperial castle, extraordinary buildings of the Burgraves of Nuremberg, and the municipal buildings of the Imperial City. The castle, together with the city walls offers a picture-perfect setting. It is a popular attraction among nature lovers and history buffs alike.

One of the most important buildings in the city is the church of St. Sebaldus, located at the Albrecht-Dürer-Platz. The church was destroyed during the Second World War and was subsequently restored. This medieval church is a major tourist attraction because of the historical significance of the area.

If you are looking for a place to keep your kids entertained, make sure to visit an open-air zoo in Nuremberg. It is located on the Schmausenbuck Hill, at the eastern edge of the city. The zoo has approximately 300 animal species, and it is one of the largest European zoos. The Dolphinarium is also located inside the zoo, and it is the first outdoor enclosure for dolphins in Germany. And remember, when your kids are happy, you can relax too.

Lindau

Lindau is a major town and an island located on the eastern side of Lake Constance in Bavaria. It is visited by thousands of tourists from across the globe. With hiking, cycling, sailing, hiking, swimming, and camping all available in beautiful surroundings, it's no wonder that Lindau is so popular. Lindau is an ideal vacation spot for the active types. The area offers a picture-perfect setting. This town has been a popular outdoor getaway for years. Sailing is a relaxing way to experience the town's natural beauty, and if you are hungry, check out any of the wonderful eateries located in the area.

From wonderful museums to breathtaking scenery, Lindau has everything you would expect, and more. With its plethora of wonderful attractions, diverse cultural heritage, and fantastic restaurants, there is no shortage of things to do and see in Lindau. If you are looking for small, quirky pieces to take home as a souvenir, look no further. Lindau has a lot of charming little vintage shops.

In 1804, Lindau was ruled by Austria and passed to Bavaria in 1805. Today this charming town is a renowned resort and tourist centre. The Sea Life Center in Constance, and Island of Mainau in the Constance Lake can be easily reached from Lindau. During the summer months, Lindau is packed with tourists and locals. This lovely town also has one of the most beautiful harbors in Europe, dominated by a 6 meter lion monument at the entrance. The town is well known for its beautiful architecture and still retains a medieval appearance.

Among the most popular landmarks are the old town hall, and St. Stephen's Church. Lindau is also just an hour away from ski resorts in Germany and Switzerland.

The Black Forest

The most popular of Germany's rural destinations is the Black Forest, whose spectacular size, is definitely eye catching. Basically, it is a great forested mountain range bounded by the Rhine valley. It is located in southwestern Germany, in the state of Baden-Württemberg. The area is perfect for walking or for just wandering around and enjoying the pretty villages nestling under the mountains or along lakeshores.

The Black Forest is Germany's best kept secret. This ancient forest is famous for its legends and myths. A blend of untamed and domesticated nature, the area is a wonderful place to go hiking or mountain biking. It also offers a few skiing resorts. The Feldberg is the highest mountain in the Black Forest. The area is famous throughout Germany and among those interested in wine. Some of Germany's best beers and wines are produced in the region. This is a fascinating area to visit, with its contrasting landscapes and beautiful villages.

The Black Forest has several rivers including the Danube, the Enz, the Kinzig, the Murg, the Nagold, the Neckar, the Rench, and the Wiese. The most popular destination in the Black Forest is Titise, a medium-sized lake with associated village. It is a peaceful place for a picnic or walk, with marvelous views.

However, the Black Forest's top attraction is the spa town of Baden-Baden. The area has a number of great restaurants, but they are quite pricey. There are also lots of fascinating shops in the area selling everything from souvenirs to locally produced crafts.

Chapter 13: Important things everyone should know

Germany is a very safe country. Compared to most other European countries crime is very low and common sense should keep you out of any trouble. Although Germany is relatively safe, make sure to keep a close watch on your valuables. There is always the possibility that something can go wrong, so you should make copies of your passport, travel itinerary and tickets, credit cards, and any other important documents. Always keep the copies in separate locations. To avoid being pickpocketed, keep your wallet in your front pocket, and do not place your credit cards, tickets, and passport all in the same place. You should always use common sense and the same precautions you would in any other country. Luckily, you won't have any trouble finding English-speakers in Germany. But, if you are looking to blend in with the locals, you will benefit from learning a few basic German phrases.

Taking an organized tour

If you dislike the idea of booking a tour, think again. Throughout the country you can find an ever-increasing number of tour companies offering all kinds of organized trips, from walking tours and one day excursions to wild adventures. And finding the right organized tour is easy and relatively inexpensive. Booking a tour can only enrich your travel experience, and some of the best attractions and hidden places can only be reached on a guided tour. Germany is one of the few countries in the world where you can experience a little bit of everything: beautiful islands, lush forests, stunning vineyards, towering mountains, breathtaking valleys, delicious cuisine, and rich heritage.

If you are spending more than a few days in Germany, a guided tour is probably the most efficient and informative way to check out some famous attractions. Some tours can take you off the beaten path and give you great insights. That being said, Germany offers expeditions and trips for every budet and interest. You can arrange day trips covering a vast range of activities in all major cities in Germany.

The country has a great variety of tours on offer. Various companies organize different tours, offering visitors interesting ways to explore the country. You can enjoy various cruises on the river. Evening dinner cruises are also offered. Let's face it, there is no better way to immerse yourself in our culture and have the adventure of a lifetime.

Chapter 14: Final Words

A trip to Germany is certainly the opportunity of a lifetime. Every country has its marvels and wonders, but Germany truly has it all. From trend-defining cuisine, iconic landmarks, stunning landscapes, world-renowned symphony and opera to almost boundless outdoor and shopping opportunities, Germany stands out as one of the ultimate must-sees on any traveler's wish list. To top it all off, Germany is a country that truly satisfies all the senses. It has something special that will keep you coming back. Whether you are in Berlin, Stuttgart or Munich, there will always be something that will capture your heart. Hopefully this book will add more value to your vacation. Have as much fun as you can and enjoy every moment.

PS: Please leave your review

If you reached this last page, probably this travel guide has given you some ideas about your stay in Germany!

Would you be kind enough to leave a review for this book on Amazon? It will help other travelers to find their way through this beautiful country!

Many thanks and enjoy your trip!

©Copyright 2018 - All rights reserved.

This document is geared towards providing exact and reliable information in regards to the topic and issue covered. The publication is sold with the idea that the publisher is not required to render accounting, officially permitted, or otherwise, qualified services. If advice is necessary, legal or professional, a practiced individual in the profession should be ordered.

From a Declaration of Principles which was accepted and approved equally by a Committee of the American Bar Association and a Committee of Publishers and Associations.

In no way is it legal to reproduce, duplicate, or transmit any part of this document in either electronic means or in printed format. Recording of this publication is strictly prohibited and any storage of this document is not allowed unless with written permission from the publisher. All rights reserved.

The information provided herein is stated to be truthful and consistent, in that any liability, in terms of inattention or otherwise, by any usage or abuse of any policies, processes, or directions contained within is the solitary and utter responsibility of the recipient reader. Under no circumstances will any legal responsibility or blame be held against the publisher for any reparation, damages, or monetary loss due to the information herein, either directly or indirectly.

Respective authors own all copyrights not held by the publisher.

The information herein is offered for informational purposes solely, and is universal as so. The presentation of the information is without contract or any type of guarantee assurance.

The trademarks that are used are without any consent, and the publication of the trademark is without permission or backing by the trademark owner. All trademarks and brands within this book are for clarifying purposes only and are the owned by the owners themselves, not affiliated with this document.

CPSIA information can be obtained
at www.ICGtesting.com
Printed in the USA
LVHW050859021218
598971LV00003B/971/P